How Should
Christians
Vote?

MOODY PUBLISHERS

CHICAGO

Editor: Christopher Reese   Cover Design: Barb Fisher, LeVan Fisher Design
Interior Design: Ragont Design Cover Photo: Zentilia / Shutterstock
Author Photo: Trey Hill

Library of Congress Cataloging-in-Publication Data

Evans, Tony, 1949-
    How should Christians vote? / Tony Evans.
       p. cm.
    Includes bibliographical references (p.   ).
    ISBN 978-0-8024-0479-4
    1. Voting—Religious aspects—Christianity. 2. Christianity and politics.
    3. Christianity and politics—Biblical teaching. 4. Christians—Political
    activity. I. Title.
    BR115.P7E93 2012
    261.7—dc23

                                    2012004950

We hope you enjoy this book from Moody Publishers. Our goal is to provide high-quality, thought-provoking books and products that connect truth to your real needs and challenges. For more information on other books and products written and produced from a biblical perspective, go to www.moodypublishers.com or write to:

Moody Publishers
820 N. LaSalle Boulevard
Chicago, IL 60610

1 3 5 7 9 10 8 6 4 2

Printed in the United States of America

CONTENTS

God's System of Civil Government

Many, if not most, Christians begin with the wrong question of *who they should vote for* rather than the more important question of *how they should vote*. Asking the correct question is fundamental to knowing how to arrive at the correct answer.

If you were to come to me with your personal life in shambles and you didn't know which way to turn, and you said, "Tony Evans, help me," I would open up my Bible, identify the cause of your personal dilemma, and speak God's truth about your situation—giving you God's resolution for whatever it is that you are facing.

If you were to come to me with your family life in shambles with both you and your spouse seeking a divorce because of chaos in your home, and you said, "Tony

Evans, help me," again I would open up my Bible, identify the cause of your familial dilemma, and present to you God's solution for whatever it is that you are facing.

If you were a pastor of a church and you came to me with your deacons or elder board because your church was in shambles, everyone was arguing, and your congregation was confused, and you said, "Tony Evans, help us," I would open the very same Bible that I used to help the individual and the family, and I would identify the cause for the chaos based on the Word of God, seeking to prescribe biblical solutions for the calamity in your church.

In other words, Scripture would not only solve the individual and family divisions, but it would also solve the ecclesiastical confusion. This is because Scripture holds the final and authoritative answer on all of life's concerns. In fact, every question facing us today has two answers: God's answer and everyone else's. And when those two differ, everyone else is wrong.

Yet where do we often go for answers as a nation when there is chaos in our country? Where do we turn for solutions when we are experiencing moral, social, and economic decline at a rate that is able to destroy our country before our youngest generation even has a chance to grow up? What do we do when divisions, debt, and our own internal protests across our land threaten what little stability we have left?

What most Christians do, unfortunately, is change books. When it comes to politics and elections, far too many Christians spend more time appealing to family, history and tradition, culture, racial expediency, and personal preference than they do to what the Bible teaches. While Scripture is good enough for individuals, families, and churches, it seems that somehow it has been deemed insufficient for how we respond to politics and government.

Yet the same book that can restore a person, home, or church is the very same book that can restore and transform our nation. Friend, we don't need to change books. In fact, it is precisely because we have changed books that the chaos in our country has gotten worse than ever before.

> # GOD IS IN CHARGE,
> # AND ALONE SITS AS THE ULTIMATE
> # GOVERNMENT OVER HIS CREATION.

It astounds me that in all of the talk permeating the airwaves, around watercoolers, over dinners, and among Christian friends concerning the elections, candidates, parties, and platforms—how little a *biblically based* theistic worldview seems to enter the equation. God may get dropped in here or there on one issue, or perhaps two. But that is not good enough. Unless God and His revealed

Word is the overarching influencer and rationale over how our electoral decisions are made as believers, then we cannot expect God to be the overarching influencer in our nation. Nor can we expect God to pour out His blessings on us as a country when He has been similarly marginalized, and at times even dismissed, from the equation.

GOD RULES

My fellow believers, it is time to return to the Book. It is time to look to the one source that holds the answers for how our country should operate, the Bible. And to do so, I want to start with the foundational principle upon which all else should rest concerning how a Christian should vote. This principle is located in the book of Romans where we read, "Every person is to be in subjection to the governing authorities. *For there is no authority except from God*, and those which exist are established by God" (Romans 13:1, emphasis added).

God is in charge, and alone sits as the ultimate government over His creation. All other governments are then to reflect His ultimate rule. It is as straightforward, and as complex, as that. Scripture tells us clearly that there is no authority apart from God. Not only that, but we read that any governing authorities put in place have been established by God. Now that doesn't mean that the people filling the positions within the governing authorities are intentionally serving God or that their decisions are in line with God— because many, if not most, are not.

But the institution of governmental authority has been created, decreed, and established by God underneath His sovereign control.

For this reason, God cannot be removed from believers' involvement or representation in government because laws are made based on belief systems. Since the Christian's belief system or worldview is to be derived from the Bible, then out of necessity it should inform our politics and therefore should inform our vote.

A quick word on sovereignty before we move on because an accurate understanding of this principle is critical to formulating a believer's worldview on voting. Sovereignty simply means that God is accountable to no one. All things are either caused by Him or permitted by Him. To acknowledge His sovereignty means to recognize His jurisdiction, along with the validity of His supremacy, over every area of life (Psalm 103:19; Romns 11:36).

What humanism often does is offer an insufficient understanding of the sovereign purpose and work of God. These systems attempt to box God into a government confined within the perspective of man. Yet when humanity is used as the starting point for interpreting and interacting with God's creation, faulty theology and sociology emerge as mankind attempts to fashion God into the image of man. As a result, socialism and communism, in particular, use government to suppress religion to such a degree as to leave the one true God out entirely.

The other extreme are those civilizations which, in the name of their religion, create bondage. Many of these "ecclesiocracies," and even so-called theocracies, in the Middle East and elsewhere allow people the opportunity to express their faith in the religion that the government has decreed as lawful—but that expression is mandated. That is not freedom. Rather, that is oppression.

Oppressive religious rule occurs when government-mandated civil religion is used to rule over people, frequently without the consent of the governed. It includes rule by mandate of an institutional religious hierarchy, and is often resisted by its subjects.

Yet God never forces obedience to His rule. As the supreme ruler, He has allowed the freedom to obey or disobey according to mankind's choices within the sovereign lines of His boundaries. The boundary lines of God's sovereignty are the non-negotiable areas He has established. It is similar to the boundary lines on a football field. In between the boundary lines on the football field, there is given the freedom to call the plays. Likewise, God has given mankind the freedom to make decisions on the field of life.

Of course, disobedient decisions will result in consequences that are oftentimes inherent in the very activity itself (Romans 1:18–32). But in His sovereignty, God has allowed mankind to serve as representatives within His governing systems, for good or for bad.

Keep in mind that God's sovereignty allows Him to even use that which is not cooperating with Him (the bad) in order to move things to where He wants them to go.

Yet while God is able to turn things around, that does

not mean that we are to intentionally disregard God's rule. Rather, as the originator of governing authorities and as the sovereign authority over all, what God has to say regarding culture, social order, and government supersedes all else and should be the basis upon which all of our decisions, as followers of Christ, are made. In other words, as a Christian, you cannot discuss government without discussing God. This is because government is a divinely ordained institution.

Problems arise when people adopt the institution of government but dismiss the divine Ruler over government. Many people want "God bless America" today. They just don't want "One nation under God." The issue is that you can't have one without the other.

God has given us the freedom to choose whether or not we will be one nation under Him—whether we will recognize His rule and operate underneath it. But with that choice comes either "God bless America," or not. God only promises to bless the nation that recognizes His authority (Psalm 33:12).

Freedom means you get to control the choice, but because God is the sovereign ruler over His creation you don't get to control the consequences. He will rule by either endorsing your choice, or He will rule by allowing you to have the consequences of a decision made against Him.

For example, those who favor the legality of abortion on demand are making a choice against God's law not to take an innocent human being's life. God has given people the freedom to disobey Him in making this choice antithetical to what He says. And He has even given our government the freedom to issue a law that makes the murder of an unborn child legal in their system.

However, God's viewpoint on the wrongful exercise of this freedom by shedding innocent blood is given to us in the book of Genesis where we read, "Whoever sheds man's blood, by man his blood shall be shed, for in the image of God He made man" (Genesis 9:6). We also read in Proverbs that God hates "hands that shed innocent blood" (Proverbs 6:17).In Deuteronomy, God curses the one who "taketh reward to slay an innocent person" (Deuteronomy 27:25 KJV). And in Isaiah 49:1 and elsewhere in Scripture, we see God clearly recognizing the child while in the womb: "The LORD called Me from the womb; from the body of My mother He named me."

When the governing representatives of the people legalize the shedding of innocent blood (as a for-profit business, nonetheless) then they have placed themselves, and those they represent, in the direct line of God's judgment. An attack on the life of another is an attack on God Himself as humanity has been made in His image (Genesis 9:6).

As a result, there is a price tag for legalizing the shedding of innocent blood. The more unborn babies are murdered in our land, the more we can expect violence in our culture as well. Because when a culture goes against God's laws, God will allow that culture to experience the consequences of the breaking of that law—in this case the resultant devaluing of life as well as the effects of that devaluing.

The real issue at hand is how God is going to respond

to a culture when the majority of the people seek to veto Him. God has made it clear that He is the ultimate authority, and everyone else is the delegated authority, for good or for bad.

The Bible tells us that we are all "under God." We read in Psalms that "The LORD has established His throne in the heavens, and His sovereignty rules over all" (Psalm 103:19). In Daniel, it says that "the Most High is ruler over the realm of mankind" (Daniel 4:17) and that "it is Heaven that rules" (Daniel 4:26).

Scripture clearly distinguishes for us in these places and in many others that God's rule operates universally over every thing, every nation, every person, and every system, whether that be political, economic, educational, or familial. Yet while there is one ultimate Ruler, there are multiple rulers who have been put in place in order to rule. That is why Paul tells us to be in subjection to the governing authorities (Romans 13:1)—plural—as we read earlier in Romans.

GOD ESTABLISHED THE FAMILY AS THE FOUNDATION OF CIVILIZATION.

The reason for the plurality in governing authorities is that the division of power provides the best environment for the fair dispersement of power underneath the ultimate ruler, God. Just like at the Tower of Babel, when mankind tried to unite in order to usurp or reach God's rulership in the heavens, God resisted their attempt at a centralized world power (Genesis 11:1–9).

It is in dividing up governing authorities that both checks and balances are put in place against evils arising within a sinful humanity such as tyranny and dictatorships. That is why our founding fathers separated the judicial from the legislative and also from the executive branches. Since God exists as both unity and diversity (Trinity), human government has been established to reflect that pattern by being unified in their purpose while being diversified in their spheres of responsibility. The division of power is the biblical and optimal way for maximizing God's position as the ultimate authority. Government cannot be all things to all people. Only God can be everything for the people. When the state seeks to adopt such a role, it is seeking to emulate God.

THE FOUR SYSTEMS OF GOVERNMENT

Under God's rule, He has created governmental systems that consist of four distinct realms: individual, family, church, and civil government—each having specific, limited spheres of responsibility and jurisdiction. Since God alone is the ultimate authority, no human government can be. The first governmental system is also the most important of all four. This is because if this form of government is out of place, then the other three will reflect it. Likewise, if this form of government is functioning properly, the other three will reflect that as well.

The first and foundational form of government instituted by God is *self-government*.[1] The goal of self-government is to govern oneself according to the principles and precepts found in God's law. When individuals are living life in light of an attitude of self-government, then there is less of a need for anyone or anything else to govern them. In Ecclesiastes, God makes it clear what the fundamental piece of self-government entails, and that is the fear of Him. We read,

> The conclusion, when all has been heard, is: Fear God and keep His commandments, because this applies to every person. For God will bring every act to judgment, everything which is hidden, whether it is good or evil. (Ecclesiastes 12:13, 14).

The next type of government that God prescribes in Scripture is *family government*. God established the family as the foundation of civilization (Genesis 1:26–28). The Bible tells us that Christ is the head of the husband (Ephesians 5:23), and the husband is the head of the wife (1 Corinthians 11:3), and that parents are the head over their children (Ephesians 6:1). Scripture goes on to lay out the governing principles in relation to the marriage covenant and family unit. The saga of the nation is the saga of its families written large.

Along with individual and family government, God has also ordained *church government*. The church leaders, as members of the *ecclesia* (the governing body set up by Jesus Christ on His behalf), are to govern matters that apply to the church and/or church members, and serve as the moral conscience of the government. This role is crucial since the progress of a nation is directly related to the state of its morality (Proverbs 14:34).

The fourth system of government instituted by God in His kingdom rule on earth is *civil government*. Civil government is that system that has been set in place to create and maintain a righteous and just environment in which freedom can flourish. It is a representative system designed to manage society in an orderly fashion. Yet it is to do so without interfering with, negating, or contradicting God's other governing agencies. Civil government is to support, not replace, the institutions of family and church government so that self-government, and therefore maximum freedom, can be experienced.

Paul emphasizes the primary purpose of civil government in the continuation of his discussion in Romans 13 when he says,

> Therefore whoever resists authority has opposed the ordinance of God: and they who have opposed will receive condemnation upon themselves. For rulers are not a cause of fear for good behavior, but for evil.

In this verse, Paul introduces us to the one overarching job of civil government that can be defined as follows: *Under God, the government is to promote the conditions for the well-being of the citizenry for good, while protecting the citizenry against the proliferation of evil.* And since civil government is to operate under God, He—and not man—must be the ultimate standard of what is good or evil. This means that politics is fundamentally an ethical enterprise based on what is right and what is wrong. Therefore Christian voting should first and foremost be a spiritual issue.

When the government successfully keeps evil in check, good can flourish. This holds true whether it means keeping the evil out that shows up in our enemies around the world, or whether it means keeping people from knocking down your front door. Government is to restrict the flow of evil while simultaneously and intentionally seeking to expand the flow of good. Everything within civil government ought to be aimed at this one primary goal.

Paul explains,

> Do you want to have no fear of authority? Do what is good and you will have praise from the same; *for it is a minister of God to you for good.* But if you do what is evil, be afraid; for it does not bear the sword for nothing; for it is a minister of God, *an avenger who brings wrath on the one who practices evil.*
> (Romans 13:3, 4, emphasis added).

When civil government attempts to do more than that, it typically ends up infringing on other divinely authorized governments (individual, family, and/or church). When the government tries to act as someone's parent and pay someone's bills while they do not work, the government has become more than the government was designed to be. The Bible says if a man does not work, he ought not to eat (2 Thessalonians 3:6–8, 10). It is not talking about when a man cannot work. It is talking about when a man won't work. If a man does not work, you do not offer him a welfare check to pay him for his irresponsibility. You don't look to the government to pay for laziness while taxing others to cover the bill.

Just as God restricts the church from giving charity to people prior to getting the family involved first (1 Timothy 5:4), likewise civil government is not to provide charity prior to the involvement of the family, church, and other local charitable entities. This is so because help is to be given by those closest related to the need who can provide both love and accountability that promotes personal freedom and responsibility. What government can do to make this happen is to create an environment for compassion to flourish. That falls underneath its task of promoting good. When this order is reversed, then the state becomes an all-encompassing promoter of federal economic dependency leading to illegitimate and irresponsible personal and corporate welfare. Limited government, however, does not mean noncaring and incompassionate government. Civil government should provide a safety net specifically and intentionally designed to produce self-sufficency and not long-term dependency.

When civil government is limited to its primary role, it maintains an environment for God's other governments to flourish, yet it does not overextend itself and those underneath it while trying to be everything to everybody while still charging taxpayers for things it does not have divine authorization to do. An overextended civil government and overtaxed citizenry limits the freedoms of individuals to pursue their calling under God, and their capacity to contribute to economic development. It also creates an environment of restriction, doubt, and hesitation, thus stifling opportunity, initiative, and ingenuity.

The primary intended outcome of a properly functioning civil government, rather, promotes a concept we often throw around lightly in our nation today—that of freedom. It is quite possible that our freedoms are often so undervalued because we have never had to experience a life without them, like so many others around the world. It is also possible that this is because we have defined freedom wrongly. Freedom can be defined as a *release from illegitimate bondage in order to make the choice to exercise responsibility in actualizing and maximizing all that you were created to be.*

The first occurrence of this concept of freedom happens in the book of Genesis in the garden of Eden when God created mankind. We read, "The LORD God commanded the man, saying, 'From any tree of the garden you may eat *freely*'" (Genesis 2:16, emphasis added). Notice that God is referenced here as "LORD God." Normally when you read the word LORD, it refers to the personal name used for God, which is *Yahweh*. *Yahweh* literally means "master, and absolute ruler."[2] It is the name God uses to reveal Himself to mankind regarding His relationship with us. The name *Yahweh* reveals God's rule in the context of His relationship with humanity.

Thus as the Ruler over Adam and Eve, God clearly delineated the boundaries of His governmental system. Whichever tree Adam or Eve wanted to eat from, they were free to eat, except one: "from the tree of the knowledge of good and evil you shall not eat, for the day that you eat from it you will surely die" (Genesis 2:17).

Notice that in the garden under God's governing rule and original blueprint for mankind, there was *maximum freedom*. From every tree in the garden, except for one, Adam and Eve had complete and unhindered freedom to partake. This freedom also included the responsibility to manage, develop, and expand the assets God had provided them, which is the essence of free enterprise.

Yet in the context of this broad-based freedom, God also legislated strictly defined boundaries that came with serious repercussions. If anyone chose to go against the boundaries God had set up, the result would be not only dire but also immediate. While people had the freedom to choose to do wrong, they could not choose to do so without suffering severe and clearly defined consequences.

In the beginning, God was the government. His model allowed for broad freedom along with narrow restrictions, followed up with both quick and severe consequences for breaking those restrictions. Yet after the fall of mankind, God transferred the carrying out of the government of mankind to men. God had set the standard for how His creation should operate and then transferred that standard of government to mankind after sin entered the world. To the degree that civil government restricts evil, mankind can experience the freedom God originally intended.

Therefore, a government patterned off of the original design of the Creator is a government that does not seek to limit humanity's freedoms, but rather promotes freedom through the declaration of clear, broad, and just boundaries along with the carrying out of immediate and acute consequences for breaking those boundaries. It is in this type of government that individuals, families, churches, and local communities are best equipped to cultivate and maintain high levels of both productivity and enjoyment so that free enterprise can flourish.

BIBLICAL JUSTICE AIMS TO PROTECT INDIVIDUAL LIBERTY WHILE PROMOTING PERSONAL RESPONSIBILITY.

While the founding fathers fought for freedom for themselves in establishing America, most were unwilling to give it to others as demonstrated by the evil of American slavery. Yet freedom is so important that we must be involved not only in fighting for it for ourselves, but also in empowering others to experience it as well. This is why the greatest demonstration of our value and appreciation for freedom is realized in diligently serving the well-being of others (Galatians 5:13). Freedom's purest form is manifested through expanding and enriching the freedom of others.

Civil government is authorized to protect and promote this freedom through maintaining what is often called, in our contemporary culture, *social justice.* However, social justice has become a convoluted term, conjuring up different meanings depending on who is speaking. It is frequently used these days as a catchphrase for illegitimate forms of government promoting the redistribution of wealth, rather than for the redistribution of opportunity where illegitimate impediments are removed, thus giving individuals the chance to maximize their potential. Likewise, social justice often favors the collectivistic expansion of civil government, which wrongly infringes on the jurisdictions of God's other covenantal institutions (family and church).

The term I choose to use instead when speaking about the government's responsibility to create an environment of justice in society is *biblical justice,* since biblical justice aims to protect individual liberty while promoting personal responsibility (Romans 14:12; Matthew 16:27; Revelation

20:11–15). Biblical justice provides society with a divine frame of reference from which to operate using Scripture as the defining template for how it is to function.[3]

The word *justice* in Scripture simply means to prescribe the right way. Since God is just (Deuteronomy 32:4) and is the ultimate lawgiver (James 4:12), His laws and judgments are just and righteous (Psalms 19:7–9; 111:7–8). They are to be applied without partiality (Deuteronomy 1:17; Leviticus 19:15; Numbers 15:16) because justice identifies the moral standard by which God measures human conduct (Isaiah 26:7). It is the government's role, then, to be God's instrument of divine justice by impartially establishing, reflecting, and applying His divine standards of justice in society (Psalm 72:1–2, 4; 2 Samuel 8:15; Deuteronomy 4:7–8)—regardless of one's economic status (Exodus 23:3, 6; Leviticus 19:15).

Biblical justice, therefore, can be defined as *the equitable and impartial application of the rule of God's moral law in society.* The one constant factor that government is to guarantee in the areas of economic, political, social, or criminal justice is the understanding and application of an established moral law within the social realm.

Civil government exists, therefore, to promote personal and collective freedom through resisting evil and overseeing the proliferation of good through maintaining a just society. When a government fails to do this either because it runs inefficiently or ineffectively, it is typically the masses who suffer as a result.

That is why it is essential for the masses, particularly

the masses who align themselves underneath Jesus Christ, to vote according to the principles and values of the kingdom of God. While this does not mean we all vote the same way, it does mean that we are unified in utilizing the same principles when we vote. Ultimately, this determines how God as Sovereign Ruler will relate to and work through those within and under the government and its systems. This is because God oftentimes relates to us based on how His representatives relate to Him.

For example, in the governmental institution of the family, a large part of how God relates to, blesses, or does not bless a family has to do with the male leader who has been assigned to cover the family. If the man is not in alignment under Jesus Christ and is himself not covered by God's care, protection, and favor, then the family will experience the consequences of this disorder.

In the book of 1 Peter, we read that a man who does not carry out his role well in relation to God's rule of love in accordance with leading his wife will have his prayers hindered (1 Peter 3:7). If his prayers are hindered, then those under his care and covering will not be the recipients of all of the blessing and favor that could be theirs as a result of their leader seeking God's face on their behalf.

Likewise, how God's representatives in civil government relate to Him frequently affects how He relates collectively to those underneath their leadership. Because this is so, it is even more important that you and I as believers make our voting decisions based on what and who best reflects God's kingdom rule (1 Samuel 8:18).

The Kingdom Agenda

Every voting choice you exercise ought to be for the candidate, platform, party, or policy that will best represent the values of the kingdom of God. The answer to how a Christian should vote is as simple, and as complicated, as that. I say that it is as complicated as that because no solitary party—Democrat, Republican, or Libertarian—fully reflects the values of the kingdom of God.

On a number of issues, the Democrats represent the values of the kingdom of God. And then on a number of other issues, the Democrats are antithetical to God's kingdom laws. Similarly, on a number of issues, the Republicans reflect the values of the kingdom of God. But then again, on other issues, they do not.

As a Christian, your responsibility when you cast your vote will be to understand the principles of God's kingdom and His values, and then compare these with the content and character of whatever person, party, platform, or policy for which you will cast your vote.

When you understand the values of God's kingdom, you will best understand His agenda.[4] However, it is my conviction that the message of the kingdom, and the values therein, are sorely lacking in understanding today. As a result, this has caused much, if not most, of the confusion in our land. Not because people don't speak of the kingdom, but because far too much of their speech is in esoteric, theological "code words" that seem unrelated to the realities of life in the here and now.

The absence of a comprehensive understanding of the kingdom has led to deterioration in our world of cosmic proportions. People live segmented, compartmentalized lives because they lack a kingdom worldview. Families disintegrate because they exist for their own fulfillment rather than for the kingdom.

Churches are having a limited impact on society because they fail to understand that the goal of the church is not the church itself but the kingdom. This myopic perspective keeps the church divided, ingrown, and unable to transform the cultural landscape in any significant way.

And because this is so, society at large has nowhere to turn to find solid solutions to the perplexing challenges that confront us today—troubling problems such as crime, racism, poverty, and a myriad of other ills that continue to show up in our politics and policies year after year. Yet for each and every issue, God's kingdom agenda provides an alternative, another way to see and live life in this world. It transcends the politics of men and offers the solutions of heaven.

I like to think of the kingdom of God as the *alternative*, because that word in particular states that there is another way, another idea on the floor. As God's people, we are not limited by the choices this world offers us. God has an alternative plan for us—His kingdom.

Throughout the Bible, the kingdom of God is His rule, His plan, and His program. God's kingdom is all-embracing. It covers everything in the universe. In fact, we can define God's kingdom as His comprehensive rule over all creation.

Now if God's kingdom is comprehensive, so is His kingdom agenda. The kingdom agenda, then, may be defined as *the visible demonstration of the comprehensive rule of God over every area of life.*

The reason so many believers are struggling is that we have voted in the past asking God to bless our plans rather than casting our votes based on seeking His agenda. We want God to sign off on our decisions rather than us following His.

But it doesn't work that way. God has only one plan, one alternative, and it is to advance His kingdom. We need to find out what that looks like so we can make sure that we are voting for God's plan, and not ours.

The Greek word the Bible uses for kingdom is *basileia,* which basically means a "rule" or "authority." Included in this definition is the idea of power. So when we talk about a kingdom, we're talking first about a king, and a ruler who has power.

Now if there's a ruler, there also have to be "rulees," or kingdom subjects. A kingdom also includes a realm: that is, a sphere over which the king rules. Finally, if you're going to have a ruler, rulees, and a realm, you also need kingdom regulations—guidelines that govern the relationship between the ruler and the subjects. These are necessary so the rulees will know whether they are doing what the ruler wants done.

God's kingdom includes all of these elements. He is

the absolute Ruler of His domain, which encompasses all of creation. And His authority is total. Everything God rules, He runs—even when it doesn't look like He's running it. Even when life looks like it's out of control, God is running its "out-of-controlness." At the heart of the kingdom agenda philosophy is the fact that there should never be a separation between the sacred and the secular. All of life is spiritual, since all of life is to come under God's rule. Therefore, every issue—whether social, political, economic, educational, environmental, or otherwise —is to mirror God's principles related to the specific area and thus reflect and promote His agenda in history.

God has made Jesus Christ the Sovereign over all mankind's kingdoms (Matthew 28:18; Colossians 1:13–18). His rule is to be represented in history by those who are a part of His kingdom and who have been delegated the responsibility of dispensing His rule to the nations (Matthew 28:19, Ephesians 1:22, 23). Christian voting should reflect this reality.

Colossians 1:13 says that everybody who has trusted the Lord Jesus Christ as Savior has been transferred from the kingdom of darkness to the kingdom of light. If you are a believer in Jesus Christ, your allegiance has been changed. You are no longer to follow the world's ways, but Christ's.

And just in case there's any doubt, there are no in-between kingdoms. There are only two realms in creation: the kingdom of God and the kingdom of Satan. You are subject to one or the other. And as a believer, you are to be subject to Jesus Christ in His kingdom. This means you belong to another realm, your allegiance is in another order, and no matter where you live, work, travel, or vote, you are a citizen of God's kingdom.

A story is told about a man who needed to get his shoe repaired. He rushed to the shoe repair shop only to arrive there at exactly 5:00 p.m. Scanning the parking lot, he noticed that it was empty, indicating that, apparently, there was no one around. Knowing he wouldn't have another opportunity to go to the shop for some time, he headed to the door to see if, by chance, it was still open.

To his surprise, the shoe repairman was there.

"I didn't think anyone was here," the man said, relieved.

"You came just in time," the shoe repairman replied. "I was almost ready to go home."

Remembering the empty parking lot, the man asked, "How are you going to go home? I didn't see any cars."

"Oh, that's easy," the repairman said. "Do you see those stairs over there?"

He pointed to the corner of the shop. The man looked and noticed the stairs. He nodded.

"I live up there," the shoe repairman said. "I just work down here."

WE LIVE UP THERE

You and I, as brothers and sisters in Christ, live up there too. "Our citizenship is in heaven" (Philippians

3:20a). That is our home. That is the kingdom to which we belong. We just work down here. Understanding this key spiritual truth is fundamental to all we do, and how we vote, on earth.

The kingdoms of this world would have us forget where our home is and lead us to believe that where we work is also where we live. But we, as members of the body of Christ, get our instructions and directions from another realm—from another King who is heading up another kingdom.

To walk into a voting booth and simply pull a lever because that is what your friends do, that is what your family does, or that is how you have always voted will be to neglect one of the greatest responsibilities you have, which is to cast a vote for the values of the kingdom of God.

Rather, your vote ought to be determined by an intentional knowledge of God's kingdom purposes on earth, combined with a thorough understanding of the issue or candidate at hand.

Then you will not only cast your votes for the betterment of your country, but you will also cast your votes for the advancement of God's kingdom.

THE SACRED
AND THE SECULAR

You cannot read the Bible and ignore the political realm. The Bible is thick with politics. You have two books, 1 and 2 Kings, that strictly deal with the rule and reign of government leaders. John the Baptist condemned the immoral conduct of Herod Antipas, which led to the prophet's execution (Mark 6:14–29). In Thessalonica, Paul and his companions were charged with committing treason against Rome for insisting "that there is another king, Jesus" (Acts 17:7). And in the greatest act of political and moral rebellion ever against God, the Antichrist will set up his worldwide government of pure evil, and he will rule the earth (Revelation 13:1–10).

Because God is the Sovereign of His universe, it follows that He is intimately concerned with the political

affairs of the nations. Psalm 22:28 declares, "The kingdom is the LORD's and He rules over the nations." There
is nothing that happens in the governments of men that
does not flow out of the sovereign rule of God. "The
king's heart is like channels of water in the hand of the
Lord; He turns it wherever He wishes" (Proverbs 21:1).

All through the Bible, we see God placing people
strategically in the political realm. He moved Joseph into
authority in Egypt (Genesis 41:38–49) and elevated
Daniel to a position of great influence among the Baby-
lonians and later the Persians (Daniel 1:8–21; 2:46–49;
6:1–3). God also placed Nehemiah in the Persian government so he could rebuild his community with government support (Nehemiah 2, 3). He made Esther queen in
Persia (book of Esther), and Deborah judge in Israel to
accomplish His agenda (Judges 4–5).

In fact, the greatest example of God's involvement in
the political affairs of a nation is Israel itself where God
established its constitution, legal structure, and laws that
were to be the model for other nations to emulate (Deuteronomy 4:5–7). Along with 1 and 2 Kings, in books such
as 1 and 2 Samuel and 1 and 2 Chronicles, God is active
on every page, setting up this king, judging that king, and
deposing yet another king. There is no escaping God's
political activity. This means we cannot divide life down
the middle, putting God on one side and politics on the
other.

Now someone may argue that while God was intimately involved in the governing of Israel, that was be-

cause God Himself established Israel as a theocracy. But when it comes to the other nations on earth, God is not that deeply involved.

Scripture would not agree with that, because in Daniel 4 we see God getting very intimately involved in the life of King Nebuchadnezzar of Babylon, the greatest secular ruler in the greatest pagan kingdom of the day.

> # GOD SITS IN JUDGMENT
> ## ON KINGS AND NATIONS.

Our look at Nebuchadnezzar begins with his over-enlarged ego that he got from spending too long gazing into his mirror. He declared himself top ruler in the universe, so God sent him a dream.

In the process of interpreting Nebuchadnezzar's dream, Daniel told him God had decreed that Nebuchadnezzar would be rendered insane until he "recognize[d] that the Most High is ruler over the realm of mankind, and bestows it on whomever He wishes" (Daniel 4:25).

But then Daniel told Nebuchadnezzar he would get his kingdom back when he thoroughly understood that "it is Heaven that rules" (v. 26). Whenever a government sets itself up as God, it is in for a short run, because there is only one King who reigns in power over the universe. God sits in judgment on kings and nations.

The rest of Daniel 4 records the fulfillment of Daniel's interpretation: Nebuchadnezzar was driven from his throne for seven years. I call this a heavenly political protest. God protested the unrighteousness of Nebuchadnezzar's government because Nebuchadnezzar sought to usurp the authority that belongs to God, which is the sin of every centralized government. Nebuchadnezzar wound up making the very confession God decreed he would make (see vv. 34–37).

The further a government drifts from God (which means it seeks to become its own god), the more it sets itself up for heavenly political action.

The greatest political statement in the Bible is the declaration of Revelation 19:16 that when Jesus Christ returns to earth to rule, He will come as "KING OF KINGS, and LORD OF LORDS." Back in Revelation 1:5, John had seen a vision of the glorified Jesus, who was declared to be "the ruler of the kings of the earth."

The Bible also says that "by [Jesus] all things were created . . . whether thrones or dominions or rulers or authorities" (Colossians 1:16). And He not only created heavenly and earthly kingdoms (v. 15), they are dependent on Him to "hold together" (v. 17) and exist by Him and for Him (see v. 16).

When Jesus was on earth, He was perceived as a political threat. At one of Jesus' trials, the Jewish council brought Him to Pilate with this accusation: "We found this man misleading our nation and forbidding to pay taxes to Caesar, and saying that He Himself is Christ, a King" (Luke 23:2). The charge that Jesus forbade people to pay taxes was simply untrue, as we will see in the discussion below. Earlier in His ministry, Jesus protested the evil of Herod's reign (Luke 13:31–32).

So to talk about the activity of God the Father and God the Son both in history and in the future is to merge the sacred with the secular in the arena of politics.

We have already argued that the sacred and the secular do mix. The question is, how do they mix?

DO WE PAY OR DO WE NOT PAY?

Jesus answered that in Mark 12:13–17. This is the incident in which the Pharisees and Herodians, normally religious and political enemies, teamed up to trap Jesus in His words.

Now you have to understand that the Pharisees and the Herodians had absolutely nothing in common. They were from two different worlds. The Pharisees were the religious conservatives of the day. They were the ones who emphasized the moral codes of the law. The Herodians, on the other hand, were all about politics. They were concerned to keep Israel on good terms with the Roman government. The Pharisees and the Herodians couldn't stand each other, but neither could they stand Jesus.

The Pharisees didn't like Jesus because He was too socially involved. They wanted Him on their side—attending Bible studies all day long, going to church and singing praise songs, while discussing the law ad nauseam. But Jesus was out healing the blind, the sick, and the lame and at times even addressing the inequities and mistreatment of women. From the Pharisees' standpoint, He was too involved in social issues and trying to right the wrongs of society. They wanted Him to just stand and preach the existing law instead.

Yet from the Herodians' vantage point, Jesus was too religious because He was telling people to repent because the kingdom of God was at hand. He was teaching about a heavenly kingdom with earthly dominion. If He just fed the poor, raised the dead, and helped the lame to walk, then maybe they could have stomached this Jesus. But since He was bringing religion into politics, they wanted it stopped.

So these two groups got together to ask Jesus a trick question concerning the separation of church and state. They figured Jesus had to take either God's side or Caesar's side, and either way He would get in trouble with somebody.

So they came to Jesus and asked, "Teacher, we know that You are truthful, and defer to no one; for You are not partial to any, but teach the way of God in truth. Is it lawful to pay a poll-tax to Caesar, or not? Shall we pay or shall we not pay?" (Mark 12:14–15a).

The question was well thought through by these men.

The trap was that if Jesus said, "Don't pay the tax because it is unlawful," which is what the Pharisees believed, then He would have been condemned for treason against the Roman state.

But if Jesus said, "Pay the tax," He would be siding with a foreign government that was oppressing God's chosen people. It was a no-win situation for Jesus as far as His questioners were concerned. They thought they had Him.

GOVERNMENT IS LEGITIMATE

But Jesus answered the question perfectly and frustrated their plot. "Knowing their hypocrisy, [Jesus] said to them, 'Why are you testing Me? Bring Me a denarius to look at'" (Mark 12:15b).

Jesus asked for a common coin of the day. The Pharisees and Herodians must have wondered where this was going, but they brought Him the coin (v. 16a).

Then Jesus asked them a question. "'Whose likeness and inscription is this?' And they said to Him, 'Caesar's.'" The image on the coin was that of Caesar, and the inscription read "Tiberius Caesar Augustus."

"And Jesus said to them, 'Render to Caesar the things that are Caesar's, and to God the things that are God's.' And they were amazed at Him" (v. 17).

These men thought they had Jesus in a trap, but He sidestepped them by saying in effect, "I don't know why you asked Me this question. You have already submitted yourselves to the authority of the Roman government by virtue of the fact that you had a denarius to give Me in the first place."

In other words, when the Pharisees and Herodians accepted Roman coins, they were recognizing Rome's governmental authority. They were using the government's money and benefiting from the government's provision. Jesus clearly stated that they were to render (to pay back for services rendered to them) to the government what was due to it.

By that I mean, if the government is providing you with protection through its military, the ability to travel on its roads, education through its schools, then you are to render back to it for its services. It is not wrong to pay taxes. In fact, it is theft not to pay your taxes because you can't have police, education, emergency services, roads, and military without paying for it. You can't benefit from it without contributing to it the portion you are responsible to pay. You are to pay that which is legitimately owed to Caesar. So Jesus was saying they should not deny the government that which was within its legitimate authority to collect, which in this case was the poll tax.

GOVERNMENT IS LIMITED

A limited civil government is not one that excludes the priority of justice functioning in society—on the contrary, it promotes it. What it does do is free up the other governments to fulfill their responsibility without being illegitimately infringed upon.

Yet Jesus didn't stop with His statement to give to Caesar what was his. He went on to make the same requirement when it came to the things of God. So the question is, what things belong to God?

Scripture is clear that everything belongs to God (see Psalm 24:1). So while Jesus' answer legitimized human civil government, it also limited human civil government. That is, you only give to civil government that which God has authorized it to be responsible for.

> # THE GOVERNMENT HAS NO BUSINESS INTERFERING WITH THE PREEMINENCE OF GOD IN OUR LIVES.

The problem comes when civil government tries to be more than it was designed to be, or fails to protect or promote that which government was designed to protect or promote (personal responsibility, family, church, and other private local expressions of charity.) Civil government was never created to be your parent. When civil government expands and reaches into the other three spheres of government God has instituted (personal, family, and church), tyranny results, reflected in high illegitimate taxation that causes civil government to grow far beyond its divinely authorized scope. This allows civil government to both confiscate and redistribute that which is not lawfully theirs, as was in the case in 1 Samuel 8 (verses 10–18).

The economic responsibility of civil government is to remove fraud and coercion from the marketplace, thus keeping it free from tyranny. It is not to control the marketplace. At best, it should seek to compete in the marketplace, demonstrating its ability to function efficiently, effectively, and for a profit rather than control the marketplace because of its size, power, or ability to print money. Centralized governmental control of trade is the economic system of the Antichrist (Revelation 13:17). All of this suggests that centralized governmental ownership or control of the ways and means of production is against God's design (i.e., socialism and communism).

Giving to God

Within its legitimate boundaries of governance, we are to give Caesar what is his. Yet Jesus also said that when it comes to giving God what is His, everything is on that list. We owe God our total obedience in every area of life. So when obeying the government will clearly prevent you from obeying God, obedience to God takes precedence. The government has no business interfering with the preeminence of God in our lives.

Today, many seek to illegitimately utilize the state to control, limit, or even silence the church's voice in the public arena. While there must be the institutional separation of church and state, there can never be a separation of God and government.

Jesus told Pilate at His trial, "You would have no authority over Me, unless it had been given you from above" (John 19:11). So even though Jesus' enemies had turned Him over to Pilate, and even though Pilate had the power to sentence Jesus to death, the authorities were only doing what God allowed them to do. The state must always recognize God's preeminence.

Now, when a government rebels against God's authority and tries to throw off His yoke, that government is going to be in trouble. When a nation's laws no longer reflect God's standard, then that nation is in rebellion against Him and will inevitably bear the consequences.

When that happens, the people of God must take action to restore God's authority and see that His kingdom agenda is carried out. This leads us naturally to our next point of consideration.

THE NATURE OF KINGDOM POLITICAL INVOLVEMENT

What is biblically based kingdom political involvement? It is involvement that recognizes that since God rules over all, the political realm must be held accountable for straying from His authority and brought back into submission to Him.

This is done not by unrighteous political revolution,

which is a change imposed from the top down, but by social transformation based on spiritual principles from the bottom up.

God is against unrighteous revolution in the sense of imposing violent governmental change from the top down, because that's what Satan sought to do. Satan tried to pull a coup d'état against God's government in heaven. He rebelled against God's leadership, but the rebellion was put down.

When a government acts unrighteously, what God wants from His people is not revolution but transformation. This involves the doctrine of interposition, which is a biblical form of protest.

INTERPOSITION

Interposition occurs when righteous agents of God advocate on behalf of those facing imminent judgment or danger.

The Bible contains many examples of interposition. When God announced to Abraham that He was going to destroy Sodom and Gomorrah, Abraham interposed himself between God and Sodom and pled with the Lord to spare the city if He could find just ten righteous people in it (see Genesis 18:16–33).

Moses's wife, Zipporah, took action when God sought to kill Moses because he did not circumcise his son. Zipporah performed the circumcision, and Moses's life was spared (see Exodus 4:24–26).

After Israel built the golden calf in the wilderness, God was angry with the people and wanted to destroy the nation. But Moses interposed himself between God and the people, and God changed His mind (see Exodus 32:1–14).

We could also cite the story of Esther in Persia, who literally laid her life on the line to spare the Jews from Haman's decree that they be wiped out (see Esther 4:1–17).

But the greatest example of interposition is Jesus Christ, who interposed Himself between a holy God and sinful people. Because of His work, the judgment that was due us fell on Him, and we were saved from destruction by God's wrath.

As Christians, we are called to act whenever unrighteousness raises its head and threatens to bring the judgment of God upon society. If Christians shun politics, there will be no one to act as a watchman (see Ezekiel 33:1–9) to warn the people of danger and to hold back the judgment of God.

We need to be like Abraham, interposing ourselves between God and an unrighteous society, pleading with God to spare the innocent and deliver our communities from His judgment. One major and intentional way we are to act in interposition is to vote according to God's kingdom values. *Every voting choice you make ought to be for the candidate, platform, party, or policy that will best represent the values of the kingdom of God.* Simultaneously, we are to seek to change the nonbiblical values that exist.

The reason interposition is so critical in the political

arena is that if righteous people do nothing, there is no reason that God should not bring judgment on a society. If His people sit on the sidelines, there are no other agents to stay the hand of God.

God calls us to interpose ourselves in this culture, to be a voice for righteousness, to stand up for the innocent, and to uphold God's righteous standard in society.

We are to show the world another option, what I call God's alternative. That may include protesting the evil that is being allowed to hold sway in a society.

There are a couple of ways to do that. One type of interposition is personal protest, based on biblical conviction, against unrighteous government action. Daniel did this as a young captive in Babylon, refusing to eat the king's meat because he did not want to break God's law and defile himself (see Daniel 1).

But Daniel did more than just refuse the food. He offered the chief eunuch another option, suggesting that he allow Daniel and the other young men to eat vegetables.

What we need in politics are godly people who will offer society a divine alternative. We need people who will stand up and say, "Your way is wrong, but let's try this way, which is God's way, and see if it makes a difference."

We don't know what would have happened if Nebuchadnezzar's eunuch had refused Daniel's recommendation. But we do know what happened when Daniel's three Hebrew brothers refused to bow to the king's image (see Daniel 3). They were sentenced to die.

The actions of Shadrach, Meshach, and Abednego illustrate another type of interposition, one that is common to our era: protest through civil disobedience. This involves deliberate personal resistance to a government law or decree that violates God's standards.

There's an interesting example of this kind of interposition in Exodus 1. This concerned Pharaoh's order to the Hebrew midwives: "If [the child] is a son, then you shall put him to death; but if it is a daughter, then she shall live" (Exodus 1:16).

But the midwives decided to disobey Pharaoh's order because they "feared God" (v. 17). In other words, they recognized that God's law was higher than Pharaoh's law, so they stepped in between the innocent Hebrew children and the king.

Their civil disobedience could have cost them their lives, because Pharaoh called them to account for letting the Hebrew male babies live. Now the midwives lied about the reason (see v. 19), but God blessed them for putting His covenant above the commands of men (see v. 20). Thus, in relation to voting, when faced with a situation where neither candidate or party appears to represent God's kingdom values, or both answers offered about policy or law are wrong, then it must be determined which answer can be best used to give God the most glory. You must choose, like the midwives, the lesser of two evils and base your decision, and your vote, and political involvement on what is in the best interest of God's kingdom.

Peter and John practiced this when the government's action was in direct violation of God's command:

And when they [the Jewish council] had summoned them, they commanded them not to speak or teach at all in the name of Jesus. But Peter and John answered and said to them, "Whether it is right in the sight of God to give heed to you rather than to God, you be the judge; for we cannot stop speaking what we have seen and heard." (Acts 4:18–20)

The apostles were saying, "You guys figure out the legality of this thing. We have a kingdom agenda to carry out."

The problem in our society is that most people fear the government more than they fear the Lord. That's true even for many Christians, because they fear the government's power to punish people and coerce them into compliance.

But we fear the wrong entity when we fear government above God. God not only deserves and demands our first loyalty, but we need to remember that government is under God and therefore is not to be made equal to Him.

See, the problem is that too many people are looking for "salvation by government." They are putting their hope in the political realm. But God warns us what happens when we put our confidence in kings (see 1 Samuel 8:9–18). There is no such thing as salvation by government (see Judges 8:22–23).

This is why Jesus refused attempts to make Him a political Savior (see John 6:15). The Democrats are looking for a Democratic savior, the Republicans are looking for a Republican savior, and the Independents are looking for an Independent savior. But God is sitting as the potentate of the universe, saying, "I am the only Savior here." The ultimate solutions to our culture's problems won't land on Air Force One.

Peter wrote, "Fear God, honor the king" (1 Peter 2:17). That is always God's order of things. Whenever a government tries to usurp the rule of God, you have a legitimate basis for protest. Man's laws can be resisted and disobeyed when they come into direct conflict with the fundamental principles of the Word of God.

APPLICATIONS OF INTERPOSITION

Let's look at a few modern-day situations in which people practiced the principle of interposition because they held God's law in higher esteem than man's law.

One instance was during the Holocaust. Christians were right to hide Jews from the Nazis, even though it was against the law. It was right because God's law forbids us from participating in murder. For Christians to do nothing as they watched their Jewish neighbors be taken away (which is what most Christians did) was to be an accomplice to murder. So it was right in those circumstances to obey God rather than to obey men.

The civil rights marches of the sixties were also legitimate because they sought to change unrighteous laws that usurped the rule of God regarding the dignity of men. Whenever you strip a human being of the dignity that is his or hers by virtue of being made in the image of God, you are violating God's standard. The civil rights struggle was about more than just human or civil rights. It was about biblical rights.

The same arguments can be made for the right-to-life movement today. The law now says it is perfectly legal to take an unborn child's life. But that violates God's higher law that says, "You shall not murder." When government violates God's law, you have the right to interpose yourself to protest that.

> WE MUST BE CAREFUL NOT TO DRAPE THE CROSS WITH THE AMERICAN FLAG.

I need to close this section with a word about a sticky issue: the use of force in protesting wrong. Some people believe force is justifiable to right a wrong, but the Bible only sanctions force when you are protecting yourself or others from violence.

The use of force is to be defensive—in other words, not offensive. We are not to use or incite violence as a way of bringing about change. We should be known as peacemakers (see Matthew 5:9).

We said earlier that unrighteous revolution is rebellion that seeks to forcibly change things from the top down. People always want to start with the president when it comes to protesting evil or getting unrighteous laws changed.

But the kind of change we are talking about rarely ever filters down from the White House. God works from the bottom up through transformation, which is why evangelism and discipleship, which seeks to change the heart, must be at the center of the church's agenda. We must be careful not to drape the cross with the American flag, thus confusing the American dream and civil religion with the kingdom of God.

So if political action is valid based on the doctrine of interposition, what can you do to right a wrong?

The first thing you can do is to take responsibility for the courses of action that are available to you.

People often say, "What difference can one person make?" Let me ask you: What difference can one spark make in a dry forest? You can make a lot of difference.

One way you make a difference is by your vote. Christians who do not vote are shunning their responsibility to be a voice for righteousness in the public square.

Your vote can be a protest against an ungodly worldview and an endorsement of biblical views. But you must be informed to cast your vote for righteousness and justice. You need to know what the values of the kingdom of God are in order to cast a vote for the party, person, or platform that best reflects those values.[1] And you need to research the candidates and issues to know where they stand and what is at stake.

I am often asked this question: "Why do I need to vote if God has already decided who is going to win or lose?"

I usually answer that by asking another question: "Why bother to pray if you know that God is going to do what He wants to do anyway?"

Of course there are things that God has decided He will do. And there are things He has decided He will not do. But in between those two lines are a whole group of things God might do, but He has decided that He will only do them in response to His people's prayers. So if you don't pray, you don't get them (see James 4:3).

There are also certain things that God is willing to do in a society, but He won't do them until we as Christians take up our responsibilities in that society. Our actions can determine which way God will move.

Someone may say, "Well, how do I know which things God will do, won't do, or might do?" The answer is, unless the Bible specifically says, you don't know, so pray about everything. Be in contact with Him about all things. Act on your responsibility at the ballot box, and pray fervently that God's righteous standards will prevail.

Another thing we need is Christians who will pursue God's calling into the political arena. There are believers out there who should be running for office. The way to clean up politics is to put righteous people into office who possess a biblical view of civil government.

This society needs people who feel God's call on their

lives to serve Him in politics. Then we will have leaders like the ones Jethro told Moses to choose: "able men who fear God, men of truth, those who hate dishonest gain" (Exodus 18:21).

These are righteous politicians, people who serve God and others with integrity. We need people at all levels of government who will take office with a kingdom perspective in view, and a kingdom agenda to pursue.

Second, teach your children that welfare begins at home. Short-circuit any idea of first looking to the government for your family's well-being. Teach them that hard work and obedience to God are the keys to success.

Families must resist any political attempt to undermine the divinely ordained role of the family, whether it is same-sex marriage, legalized abortions, indiscriminate welfare, etc. Families must remove themselves from government dependency for support.

Third, the church should be leading the way in educating the culture concerning how to vote because it is the only entity that can interject a kingdom agenda into all the issues of the culture. The job of the church is to educate God's people to look at life from a divine kingdom perspective, and to confront the government when it strays from or contradicts God's kingdom principles. The church alone possesses the keys of the kingdom (Matthew 16:18–19), giving it divine authorization to represent His perspective in history. When the church fails to fulfill this prophetic role of confronting God's people and the culture with His unchanging standards based on His Word, then we become co-conspirators in the devolution of the culture, since God determines much of what He is going to do or not do in society based largely on how effectively He can work through His people (2 Chronicles 15:3–6; Ephesians 3:10).

The church has to do more than make people feel good about their personal walk with God. The church must give God's people a divine orientation on every subject, including politics and government. Why? Because everything the Bible speaks about, it speaks about authoritatively. And the Bible speaks to every issue of life. This means that the church should seek to reflect the kingdom of God in the realm of politics.

There is no area of life that does not have a biblical worldview attached to it. God lamented in Isaiah 5:13, "My people go into exile for their lack of knowledge."

Another thing the church should do is to create opportunities for people to become informed and involved politically. This could include offering the opportunity for voter registration. The church where I pastor holds informational meetings concerning issues that are being considered for a vote. We do these not to promote a political party, since the kingdom of God transcends the partisan politics of men, but to look at parties and issues from a kingdom perspective, so we can inject a kingdom agenda and consciousness into the political arena.

Most importantly, the church must be faithful in its role of doing good works for the benefit of society at large (Matthew 5:16; Galatians 6:10). We cannot complain about the size of big civil government when the church is having limited influence and impact in society. The welfare state would have never needed to grow as large as it has if the church had been fulfilling its role in the areas of racial justice and charity. Christians are partly to blame for the size of government we complain about. Limited church social impact will inevitably result in the expansion of civil government.

Let me show you something about prayer. One of the things we should be doing in prayer is making suggestions to God. Moses did this in Exodus 32:11–14 when he asked God not to destroy the Israelites.

You say, "Why do I need to suggest things to God?" Because it means that you have thought through what you are praying about and you have some ideas about what needs to be done rather than just sitting around doing nothing, waiting for answers to drop from heaven.

Moses not only prayed, he offered suggestions to God. God may not act on your suggestions, but it is a way of offering yourself to God to take action if He chooses to empower you for that action. It was this activity of prayer that brought an end to the evil of racial segregation as the church marched in the civil rights movement.

Finally, the church must model righteous actions through good deeds so that civil government can see the kingdom of God at work.

Righteous Leadership

Our government is in desperate need of people who can inject righteousness and justice into our political bloodstream, for a society can never rise above the quality of its leadership.

Yes, church and state are functionally separate and distinct institutions with specific spheres of responsibility and jurisdiction (2 Chronicles 26:16–19). But the idea that the church has nothing to say about how society is governed is wrong simply because all law has a religious foundation. There can be no separation of religion and state since civil government is answerable to God.

The church's job is to make sure that the state doesn't lose sight of the truth that God rules and that there is a moral standard in which the political realm must operate. The state needs to recognize and protect the church's freedom to exercise its prophetic role of being a voice for God and His righteous standards, since government is a divinely authorized institution and only God is autonomous —not civil government.

Then and only then will God's kingdom agenda for society be manifested. Accomplishing that agenda requires that all of God's people get involved politically at some level, and at a minimum, that includes your informed vote.

IS GOD A DEMOCRAT OR A REPUBLICAN?

One of the most well-known phrases in the English language occurs in our very own Declaration of Independence. In the definitive statement of freedom by those escaping oppression and monarchic rule, key values were proclaimed and preserved through these words. We read,

> We hold these truths to be self-evident, that all men are created equal, that they are endowed by their Creator with certain inalienable Rights, *that among these are Life, Liberty and the pursuit of Happiness.* (emphasis added)

This phrase outlining our inalienable rights as "Life, Liberty and the pursuit of Happiness" is one of the most widely recognized statements in our written history.

The reason why it has not become lost in the dusty annals on our shelves is because its profundity resonates intrinsically within each of us. It communicates not only with our minds, but also with our souls. It speaks of the destiny and purpose that God has planted within each of us as His treasured creation. Not only that, it shouts loudly concerning God's foundational tie to the inception of a government designed to protect the freedoms of those governed. When God is removed or diminished, then our undeniable rights are in jeopardy.

Yet what is unfortunate today is that we have somehow moved away from this foundation. We have distanced, and in some cases removed, ourselves from the basis for who we are and why we were created as a nation. We have strayed from the prescribed foundation that our government was designed to defend against the threats to, as well as to promote and increase the opportunities for, our basic inalienable rights. And instead, as believers, we have lost ourselves in a whole other question: Is God a Democrat or a Republican?

This is largely due to the reality that our political battles today revolve less around principles, or even the policies to foster those principles, than they do around politics. Democrats and Republicans have become deeply split by particular political orientations, oftentimes ushering in deadlock for the sake of deadlock. This results in the same productivity level you would achieve on a football team where five players rushed toward one goal line and the remaining six players on the team rushed to the other. As such, we as a nation are suffering underneath the spending of an inordinate amount of money as reflected in our national deficit and debt, with little forward progress to show for it.

Where does God fall on this issue of partisan politics? Is God a Democrat or a Republican? Whose side is He on?

The reason why the answer to that question is compelling is that the answer will affect the way His followers should vote.

As a believer and a child of the King, to consider casting a vote for someone or for something that would go against what God would vote for ought to be out of the question. Knowing God's viewpoint on important issues —whether it is immigration, taxation, racial disparity, abortion, social justice, or even simply partisan politics— should be one of your primary concerns as you head into any voting season.

Whose Side Are You On?

To begin, though, we must first discover whose side God is on. In order to do so, we need to turn to a battle that took place under Joshua's military and governmental leadership. In Joshua chapter 5, Joshua had crossed into the Promised Land and was now serving as the one in charge over the nation of Israel. Although God had declared that He would give the land to the Israelites, His promises needed to be made manifest through certain processes. In other words, what God had promised needed to be actualized through different battles, conquests, and wars.

One of these battles that took place happened at the city of Jericho. Now, when I mention the Battle of Jericho, you can most likely recount certain aspects of the battle, such as the armies marching undefended around the city, the priests blowing the trumpets, and the walls falling down. But there is one critical scenario that took place just near Jericho that is frequently ignored in our Bible lessons, or even in our sermons. And yet this critical scenario sheds a revealing light on how a Christian should vote.

Prior to the battle and like any military leader should, Joshua performed reconnaissance. Facing what appeared to be an impregnable wall and an invisible culture, Joshua set out to determine how best to secure his victory. As Joshua prepared to go to war against the city of Jericho, a representative of God's army approached him. Joshua then asked him a very practical and strategic question. I'll paraphrase:

"Whose side are you on? Are you on our side or are you on their side?" Or, as we might phrase it in light of our discussion, "Are you a Democrat or a Republican?"

What happened next is a game-changer. The commander of the Lord's army gave what is one of the most politically insightful principles in Scripture when he replied, again in the Evans' translation,

"Neither. I'm not on your side and I'm not on their side. I'm on God's side."

We read,

> Now it came about when Joshua was by Jericho, that he lifted up his eyes and looked, and behold, a man was standing opposite him with his sword drawn in his hand, and Joshua went to him and said to him, "Are you for us or for our adversaries?" He said, "No; rather I indeed come now as captain of the host of the LORD" (Joshua 5:13, 14).

The captain of the host of the Lord made it clear that he hadn't come to take sides. He had come to take over. He was not on Joshua's side, yet neither was he on Jericho's side. However, Joshua could have easily assumed that he would have sided with him, since Joshua was on the side of the chosen people of God. After all, that would make sense. Yet the captain made it clear: He was on God's side.

He did not align himself with Joshua's agenda nor with Jericho's. He aligned himself with a whole other agenda, that of God's kingdom. Sometimes that would play out in Joshua's favor, as in the battle at Jericho. Yet sometimes that would not play out in favor of Joshua, as we read just a chapter later in the battle of Ai. The reason the Israelites were defeated at Ai wasn't because God took the side of Ai. It was, again, that God took His own side—His own kingdom side—and Joshua's people had gone against it (Joshua 7).

GOD DIDN'T COME TO TAKE SIDES; HE CAME TO TAKE OVER.

When people ask you how you are going to vote in any upcoming election, your answer shouldn't be, "I'm going to vote with this side" or "I'm going to vote with that side." Your answer ought to be, "I'm voting with God because He has His own side. I am going to vote for the party, person, or platform that best represents God's values to advance His kingdom." God is not merely a God of Democrats. Nor is He merely a God of Republicans. God does not ride the backs of either donkeys or elephants. Like the captain of the Lord's army, God didn't come to take sides; He came to take over.

One of the best ways that I can illustrate this is through football. Now, if you know anything about me at all, you know that I love football. My son Jonathan and I serve the Dallas Cowboys together as team chaplains. It is always one of the highlights of my week meeting with the players or watching them take to the field.

In every football game, two teams battle head to head in combat in order to win a victory. For sixty minutes they war against each other in order to declare to the world which team is the greatest. But what most people don't recognize is that in every football game, there aren't just two teams out on the field. In fact, in every football game taking place in every football stadium throughout our land, there are three teams who participate.

There is the home team.

There is the visiting team.

And then there is the team of officials.

Two of the teams in this battle have the same desire—to win. But in order to win, they have to go after different goals. These two teams use various strategies and various plays to try to accomplish their goal.

Yet in the middle of everything, there is a team of men wearing black and white jerseys whose role it is to govern this war. This third team doesn't take sides with either of the teams in the battle. If they did, they would be disqualified from what they have been put there to do.

This third team is not committed to either team—rather, they owe their allegiance to a higher entity: the League Office of the NFL. This league office has set forth the rules, guidelines, and regulations by which both teams are to carry out their battle. It is the job of the third team to operate in the midst of these competing parties to carry out the intentions and governance of the NFL.

Whatever this third team decides and says overrules both teams. This is because this unique group has an allegiance that holds an ultimately greater office of authority than the two competing parties.

Yet if an official happened to be too much of a fan of one of the two teams so that his allegiance kept him from being an objective official on the field, thus not representing the larger umbrella under which he was to operate, he would have compromised his position. Likewise, if an official chose to rule apart from the governances and guidelines of the league office of the NFL, he would not be backed by the authority of that office. His authority to influence is only as strong as his alignment with that which sits above him.

One of the great tragedies in the church of Jesus Christ today is that we have lost our ability and authority to be an influence on those around us. We have lost this because we have divided and aligned ourselves with the politics of men. We have allowed the realities of politics to erect a division between us. Rather than be the third team with the power from and allegiance to a whole other King and kingdom, believers have taken sides with the two teams on the field. Believers have allowed political expedience to override the kingdom of God.

Yet, until we see each other as members of the same team—the third team— representing the same kingdom, and thus respond by intentionally embracing our oneness of purpose, we will continue to fill the airwaves of society's conscience with a cacophony of chaos rather than with the liberating cadence of truth.

God has not given His allegiance to any party. His

allegiance belongs to Himself—His Word, principles, and truth. As a follower of Jesus Christ, you represent His kingdom as well in whatever political capacity you choose to position yourself.

That does not mean that it is wrong to be a Democrat or that it is wrong to be a Republican. It just means that you may need to be—like the diet soft drinks—Democrat Light or Republican Light. In other words, no group can have your total loyalty because you belong to another team.

Since neither party takes the position that the only way to approach all the issues is from a divine perspective, you will need to base your voting decisions case by case. You may vote Democratic, *sometimes*. Or you may vote Republican, *sometimes*. Or you may vote Independent, *sometimes*. You must also seek to challenge and correct the non-biblical beliefs and policies of candidates and parties with which you are affiliated when they contradict a biblical worldview, thus fulfilling your obligation to be salt and light in the realm of politics (Matthew 5:13–16).

Frequently when I'm with other African-Americans, and the conversation of politics comes up, many will assume that I am a Republican because of my friendship with former President George Bush and the positions I take on life, marriage, and limited government. Yet when I am with many Anglos, it is often assumed that because I am an African-American and emphasize justice in society that I must be a Democrat. So, naturally, I get asked a lot, "Tony Evans, what are you?"

My answer is always the same: "I vote according to what God says on the matter." If that means the issue is abortion, then I vote pro-life (whether that be Republican or Democrat). Yet if the issue is justice, then I vote for justice (whether that be Democrat or Republican). It all depends on what we are talking about and what is being voted on.

For example, the reason why abortion-on-demand is unilaterally wrong is because it is the taking of a life. When you take someone's life, you also take away their right to liberty and their pursuit of happiness. If you take someone's life, you also take their dream, their future, their family, their career, and their children away from them. All other rights are lost when you take away the right to life.

> # YOU SHOULD VOTE FOR EACH ISSUE ACCORDING TO YOUR BIBLICALLY INFORMED CONSCIENCE.

Because of my stand against abortion, I will frequently get invited to speak at pro-life rallies or events. Yet I always ask them, "Are you sure you want me to come and speak?"

To which they reply, "Yes, you are pro-life, aren't you?"

To which I tell them, "Yes, I am. But if I am going to speak on preserving life in the womb, I am also going to speak on justice for that life after the womb, and to the tomb." This is because you don't just stop defending that person's rights after nine months. God is a God of whole life, not term. He is pro-life from the womb to the tomb.

POLITICS AND THE KINGDOM OF GOD

The problem is that none of the politics of men fully represents the kingdom of God, so you can never cast a truly pure vote. Your vote must be determined by the issues at hand. And you should vote for each issue according to your biblically informed conscience. Because each of us is at a different place in our spiritual growth and life experiences, and we all come from different backgrounds, histories, and environments, that means that not everyone is going to vote identically or prioritize the issues the same.

This requires that there be a visible demonstration of love within the church before the watching world (John 13:35), rather than a spirit of condemnation among believers who have differing political alliances. It also means that when we speak truth to the culture we must do so compassionately so it is inexplicably clear that while we maintain God's standards we do so in an attitude of humility, love, and forgiveness. While we must reject abortion we must love the woman seeking one. While we must reject homosexual marriage, we must love and minister to the homosexual. When love is detached from truth, truth loses the influence it was intended to have.

One problem is that many of those who would oppose the marches for civil rights would call on Christians to march against abortion. We must also make sure that our compassion and values apply to everyone, and not just to those we choose.

Depending on the variety of issues at hand, Christians may end up voting for different parties or candidates. However, when Christians exit the voting booth, those differences should be set aside as we work together to focus on advancing God's kingdom. We must not let the partisan politics of men determine how Christians relate to each other or how we work together to further God's kingdom. Yet, very rarely will I see Christians come together to promote God's whole-life agenda, which includes justice for the baby in the womb as well as justice for the life to the tomb.

Think of the impact we could have as the body of Christ if we would seek to advance God's kingdom through unity of function.[1] Simply defined, biblical unity is oneness of purpose. Unity is not uniformity. Unity means moving together toward the same goal. If every player on a football team was a running back, the team wouldn't accomplish their goal of scoring touchdowns. Likewise, God created each of us with unique strengths and abilities. It is when we merge these strengths and abilities together toward a common purpose that we live out true unity.

Christians must determine what God's common purpose is on every issue and join together to advance His kingdom principles regarding that area. The clearest example of this was told to me by Billy Graham when I was spending some time with him at his home one afternoon. In his typical dignified fashion, Billy Graham leaned toward me in his chair and shared with me his frustrations on how churches would come together for the sake of evangelism, but then go back to their own corners of disconnectedness after the event was over. If these churches were kingdom-minded, their impact in their communities for the kingdom of God could have been ongoing. Unfortunately, we've allowed the separation in politics to create a separation in the church as well. And because of that, we are making little visible difference in the culture at large.

So when someone asks you whether you are a Democrat or a Republican, the real answer should be, "What issue are we talking about?" Because the issue that you are talking about will determine how you vote. Not only that, we need to be careful not to judge the voting of others in the body of Christ, which fosters an atmosphere of division rather than unity. God's kingdom values must be represented in every party. This means that Christians are not to be defined by man's labels of conservative, liberal, and moderate but rather by the label *kingdom men and women.* Our designation transcends those that the society is limited to. This is why it is critical that kingdom-minded Christians are represented in every political

party—so that no matter what party is in power there is
a remnant of God's people who will keep before the party
in power the standards of God while simultaneously uniting with other believers in other parties to promote God's
kingdom agenda nationally. No one party should own the
Christian vote or be in a position to take it for granted.

Scripture is no stranger to the divisions we frequently
see among the church today, and speaks clearly to us concerning it. In Romans, we read about the differences between the Jews and the Gentiles. Both groups came from
entirely different worlds, different backgrounds, different
histories, and with two different belief systems. Yet when
they got saved, they were brought into one body that was
called the church.

Even though they now belonged to Jesus Christ, they
kept their different backgrounds and histories—and even
their different value systems in many ways. But they were
to function as a part of the family of God.

In chapter 13 of the book of Romans, Paul reminds
all of us that we are to be in subjection to our governing
authorities, as we have seen. He writes, "Therefore it is
necessary to be in subjection, not only because of wrath,
but also for conscience' sake" (Romans 13:5). The last
phrase of that statement offers us a critical factor in casting our votes and in fellowshipping with others who may
vote differently—our conscience. The *conscience* is our internal warning system. It tells a person what is right or
wrong. Guilt is produced as a result of someone violating
their conscience. All of us have a conscience. Yet like our

souls that have been distorted because of sin, our conscience is also distorted when we come to salvation in Christ. It is through the process of sanctification that a conscience becomes clearly focused on the things of God as it is educated by Scripture.

None of us has the same conscience. We are all on different places on the path toward sanctification. For example, Paul shows us in chapter 14 of Romans that the Jews and the Greeks had different belief systems that influenced their conscience. We read,

> One person has faith that he may eat all things, but he who is weak eats vegetables only. The one who eats is not to regard with contempt the one who does not eat, and the one who does not eat is not to judge the one who eats, for God has accepted him. Who are you to judge the servant of another? To his own master he stands or falls; and he will stand, for the Lord is able to make him stand. . . . But you, why do you judge your brother? Or you again, why do you regard your brother with contempt? . . . So then each one of us will give an account of himself to God. (Romans 14:2–4, 10, 12)

These two groups were different because they came from different backgrounds with different worldviews. The Jews wouldn't eat pork because that is how they were raised. The Gentiles, on the other hand, loved to eat pig-feet, chitlins, and hog-maws. They didn't have a problem with eating pork because their background and history gave them a different point of view.

Yet these differences had caused division within the body of Christ so Paul sought to address it. Today's body of Christ contains within it many differences as well. Depending on how a person was raised—whether with an environment of justice, injustice, family health, family dysfunction, lack, or plenty—this can affect the formation of a worldview. And much of that shows up in the voting booth.

Yet Paul makes clear that in issues of opinion or preference, we are not to judge one another. This doesn't mean that there is no right or wrong. God has set forth a standard of right and wrong. But outside of His established overarching laws, each person is free to follow his or her opinion as long as it does not disagree with or oppose God's overarching laws.

When it came to eating meat, the Jews were free to abstain. The Gentiles were free to eat. Yet neither was free to condemn the other for what they did.

Neither the Democratic party nor the Republican party fully represents the values of the kingdom of God. The church represents God's kingdom party. Therefore, while each person in the body of Christ is free to vote according to his or her biblically informed conscience, they are obligated to only function according to God's kingdom agenda. Keeping politics from dividing Christians along racial, cultural, social, or denominational lines keeps God's independent kingdom party strong.

Civil Government
Intruding on the Church

Most people today assume that the issues facing our nation are fundamentally political. Based on that assumption, they approach voting with the attitude that one political party needs to be removed and the other instituted more strongly.

While what America is facing today may have political aspects, it is really a spiritual decay occurring in our culture. Take for example one of the most deadly and debilitating diseases of our lifetime—HIV/AIDS. Technically, AIDS never killed anyone. What AIDS does is weaken the immune system so that the body cannot fight back and thus loses its ability to repel common bacteria and viruses that can harm it.

The reason we are facing so many issues in our culture today and in our politics is because the evil of our land has been allowed to penetrate the immune system of our nation. This is because the immune system is predicated on the strength of God's perspective, since God reigns and rules over all. When this perspective is undermined and therefore weakened, cultural colds become society's sickness.

Yet if large numbers of people who make up our society are not followers of Christ anyway, then how does God's perspective permeate our culture? Naturally, this is to take place through the influence and impact of those who make up His body—the church.

Because we so frequently fail to disciple fully through a holistic approach to Christian faith and practice, we have encouraged and even enabled the removal of God's influence within His own church, thus limiting its impact on society.

In America today, we are witnessing what looks like the devolution of a nation. We are eyewitnesses to the disintegration that is occurring on all levels and subsequently undermining what used to be known as American exceptionalism. Yet even though historically America has had major flaws in areas where it has failed the citizenry, nevertheless it was an experiment in history that was unique and subsequently produced unique outcomes.

But in the days in which you and I live, America is quickly becoming a far different nation than it ever was before. In order to stop a disease from progressing, you must first identify its cause. You need to uncover what the root of it is and from where the problem has come.

The root of the problem facing us today—showing up in the schizophrenic, or oftentimes anemic, voting of the body of Christ—reflects what the prophet Ezekiel spoke concerning the Israelites in his day.

Ezekiel's words, found in chapter 43, addressed the return of the glory of God to the temple. Keep in mind, there is only one way that God can return to His temple, and that is if He has left His temple. In other words, God had left the building. The Israelites could not locate Him because His glory had departed from the culture—particularly from the place of worship where His glory had previously resided.

As a result of God's absence there was chaos in the land. There was an increase in crime, social deterioration, and a lack of order.

Yet within Ezekiel's announcement of God's return, he also revealed why God had originally left. He said,

> He (God) said to me, "Son of man, this is the place of My throne and the place of the soles of My feet, where I will dwell among the sons of Israel forever. And the house of Israel will not again defile My holy name, neither they nor their kings, by their harlotry and by the corpses of their kings when they die, by setting their threshold by My threshold and their door post beside My door post, with only the wall between Me and them. And they have defiled My holy name by their abominations which they have committed. So I have consumed them in My anger. Now let them put away their harlotry and the corpses of their kings far from Me; and I will dwell among them forever." (Ezekiel 43:7–9)

God said that the human kings (the government) had been allowed to put their throne next to His throne and intrude their rule on His rule. So He left. God made it quite clear that His house was to have only one throne—His. But Israel had put two kings in His house and started treating them both like equals. They had allowed politics to interfere with His rule in His house. Or in terms of our day, they had allowed classism, partisan politics, racism, narcissism, secularism, humanism, and the like to intrude on His viewpoint and His rule—in His house.

And because of that, God's glory had departed. God's covering had departed. His influence, power, protection, and guidance had departed because Israel had raised up another throne as equal to His own. The team of officials had joined with the competing teams on the field.

God's glory did not return to the temple until the Israelites kept what was sacred—until they "put away" that which had intruded on God's rule and God's reign from God's own house. Instead of bringing civil religion into the church, or using the church to advance a political cause rather than the kingdom of God, God wants the church to act as a vehicle for His rule, laws, and glory.

THE CHURCH IS TO BE THE KEY TO THE TRANSFORMATION OF THE CULTURE.

It is not the Democrats' view *and* God's view in the church. Neither is it the Republicans' view *and* God's view in the church. It is not their rule *and* God's rule in His house. God rules. Yet the problem today is that far too many churches have been corrupted by civil religion, and have failed to distinguish the difference between partisan politics and the kingdom agenda.

And because the church has lost its own conscience in many ways, it has failed in its calling to be a conscience for society not only through the voting of its members, but through their own daily governance in their personal lives and families. We have allowed what the majority gives us in our media, music, schools, policies, and philosophies to infiltrate and infect the church.

The church is to be the key to the transformation of the culture, not the other way around. In the past, the church has effectively influenced the society in many ways. In fact, it was because of the emphasis on the freedom of religion, as promoted by the body of Christ, that America was born. It was also because of the promotion of freedom and equality for all, in large part through the church, that civil rights for African-Americans was achieved. In both cases, the church went against the grain of what was commonly accepted in the culture.

Yet for the church to exist as the catalyst for transformation that it was created to be, it has to maintain its independence from civil religion. In order to fulfill its divinely ordained responsibility of offering both salt and light to a world in darkness, the church must not allow civil religion or the culture to separate it from relating to the political realm from a comprehensive kingdom value system. The body of Christ is not a democracy to be influenced by the opinions of the majority. The church is

God's legislative agency in history, and is to be governed by His Word and reflect and promote that governance in every area of life. Christians operating under the kingdom agenda and bringing that influence through the church into the culture and government institutions thus promote the freedom that God wants us to experience. In fact, the church could influence through uniting and offering up its own party candidate.

THE TYRANNY OF THE 51 PERCENT

One of the greatest dangers facing us as a nation today is what appears to be a shift in our thinking and approach to governance toward that of a democracy—majority rule and majority influence. A democracy is not ideal simply because a democracy basically states that we will be governed by what the 51 percent say, which is fine if the 51 percent are right. But when the 51 percent are wrong, then everyone else falls under the tyranny of the 51 percent.

Many people do not realize this, but America is not a democracy. America is a republic. We are a constitutional republic. In fact, our constitution does not even mention the word "democracy" one time. The founders of our nation were well aware of the inequalities present in democracies, and because of this they deliberately did everything they could in drawing up our constitution to prevent us from being or becoming one.

The danger of a democracy lies in its path toward ei-

ther tyranny or "mobocracy" wherein the 51 percent en-
force mob-like rule on the others. A constitutional republic is the biblical form of government that God gave
to Moses (Exodus 18:17–27) and that was adopted by the
founding fathers as the best way to maintain an ordered
society through a bottom-up, and not top-down, system
designed to meet the legitimate needs of the people. In a
constitutional republic, the people rule through their chosen representatives who are to reflect the standards of
God in their leadership.

In a republic, the people exercise rulership, as well as
the people's representatives. Yet positioned above that
rule in a constitutional republic is the constitution itself.
Through this constitution, the powers of the government
are thus limited to the original intent and wording of the
constitution. Which means that the 51 percent cannot
vote out God's agenda for limited, just, and righteous civil
government in order that His other three realms of government (personal, family, and church) may not be infringed upon.[2] When government becomes too weak to
protect against intruders or too powerful in overtaking
too many aspects of life, it becomes a threat to the very
nation that it stands to govern.

God's intention for civil government, as reflected in the
dispersement of power present in a constitutional republic, protects and promotes true liberty and freedom. This is
because it is in defining government as such that God's
overarching rule has the capacity to be made manifest. If,

that is, His people vote in representatives and laws that reflect His will.

Scripture clearly states the role of the believer in the midst of society:

> You are the salt of the earth; but if the salt has become tasteless, how can it be made salty again? It is no longer good for anything, except to be thrown out and trampled under foot by men. You are the light of the world. A city set on a hill cannot be hidden; nor does anyone light a lamp and put it under a basket, but on the lampstand, and it gives light to all who are in the house. Let your light shine before men in such a way that they may see your good works, and glorify your Father who is in heaven. (Matthew 5:13–16)

Our job as Christians is to infiltrate where the bacteria of unrighteousness and darkness have permeated and made themselves at home. It is our job to act as salt and light in both parties and offer the kingdom's point of view. One way you do this in a constitutional republic is through your vote.

WEIGHING THE ISSUES

Again, Christians will vote based on the weight they give to specific issues. Some will say that the right to life trumps all other issues because it is the foundational right. If you take away someone's life, you take away everything else that they could seek to have in their life. So in that sense, it is a foundational issue.

However, what many people do is make it the only issue—which it is not. The commandment not to kill, given to us in the Old Testament, was one of Ten Commandments. Likewise, when Christ came as a fulfillment of the law, He gave us two overarching commandments under which all else falls: To love God, and to love others. While the right to life falls under both, so do a multitude of other issues primarily relating to matters of justice and equity.

Because of this, and because many people and their ancestors have suffered under injustices and disparities— perhaps even leading to the point of increased suicides, homicides, and criminal activity, which affect the ability for many to have and experience life—the sum total of other issues may carry more weight for them (as long as there is no governmental mandate or command to abort.)

Some voters will generalize the right to life and neglect to realize that there are some Democrats who are decidedly pro-life while there are Republicans who are decidedly pro-choice. And there are some Independents who are one or the other

So in answer to the question posed as we entered this chapter, Is God a Democrat or a Republican?, the answer is, He is neither.

Regardless of which way you vote, or regardless if you split your votes between two or even three parties, you are to function as neither as well because you are to be like the team of officials on the field. You represent another King from another kingdom and sometimes His laws will be reflected in one party and sometimes they will be reflected in another. However that looks from case to case, your allegiance belongs to Him.

Not too long ago, my son Jonathan was playing football with the Buffalo Bills when I got a call about a month before the game they had scheduled against the Washington Redskins to come and speak at their chapel service. The coach called me up and said, "Evans, will you come and do the chapel for us when we play the Redskins?" Of course I said yes.

Now, the irony of that invitation is that not too long afterwards I got another call from another NFL team to conduct another chapel—not on the same day, but on the next day. And yes, you guessed it—it was from the coach of the Washington Redskins. Again, I agreed to do it.

At that time, both the coach for the Redskins and the coach for the Bills were Christians. Both wanted to win. And both wanted me to come and speak to their teams before the game.

So whose side was I on?

Was I going to give a terrible chapel message to the Redskins because my son Jonathan was playing for the Bills? No, because I stood at both chapels as a representative of another kingdom. In spite of the fact that the two kingdoms were about to face off in war against each other, and in spite of the fact that at that moment in time I personally favored the team that my son played on, I represented a higher authority with a higher agenda.

Friend, God has called you to stand higher than the battle and above the fray. He has called you to make your decisions by His Word and not by the words of man. For example, on one side we hear that "a rising tide lifts all ships." And that is positive news—if you have a boat. But if you don't have a boat, as many on the other side argue, then you will drown in that same tide.

There are multiple issues to consider when voting. There are not only justice issues but there are moral, economic, military, racial, familial, and life issues. As we read in the book of Psalms, "Righteousness and justice are the foundation of Your throne" (Psalm 89:14). That means that both righteousness (doing right, e.g., defending the right to life in the womb) and justice (maintaining justice, e.g., promoting the right to life to the tomb) are both equally valued. We must value life, but we must also value justice in and to the lives that are here on earth.

Life ought to be the basis for all of our decisions. This is because it serves as the fundamental piece in all of the categories for consideration when it comes to voting: individual, family, church, and society.

Therefore, the three institutional governments (family, church, society) should always promote personal government, which begins by viewing all aspects of life according to God's plan. There must be a primacy in voting for that which protects and promotes personal freedom and responsibility. Because it is the foundation for all else, every issue and candidate should be viewed against the backdrop of how they, or it, promote personal self-government.

Second, because family is another of God's institutional governments, every issue and candidate should be chosen based on that which strengthens or enhances heterosexual marriage and the family structure as God has designed it.

Your vote matters.
Never treat your vote lightly.

Third, in order to enable the church to function in the institutional role that God has ordained for it, every issue and candidate should be considered in light of how they can best keep civil government from intruding on the church and the freedom of religion, while simultaneously recognizing and respecting the church's role of being the divinely ordained conscience of society.

Last, every vote that pertains to the sphere of civil government should be chosen based on the ability of the candidate or policy to promote civil government in such a way that it will support the other three governments (personal, family, church), rather than infringe upon them.

Likewise, candidates and policies that create a just environment for freedom to flourish should be preferred.

Your vote matters. Never treat your vote lightly.

Don't merely look at what the Democrats say, or at what the Republicans say. Think like a kingdom citizen as you sift through issues and candidates, and consider what God says in His Word about the matter. Then use that as the basis for how you cast your votes. Vet the candidates based on their competence, how closely they are aligned to Scripture, as well as the quality of their character and reputation (Exodus 18:21). The key categories, as I just mentioned, that you should focus on when casting your votes are those that pertain to the individual, family, church, and civil government. Within those categories, the key issues that you should prioritize in your kingdom perspective and biblical view are life, freedom, justice, and righteousness as God defines them. We should desire to maximize freedom for people to responsibly and safely live their lives and pursue their calling under God.

As a Christian, it is your job to promote God's kingdom values and stand in the divide without giving full allegiance to any one party. You are to model yourself after God—the consummate independent who always votes for Himself. As such, you are to cast your votes according to that which most closely reflects, represents, and promotes the principles, values, and agenda of the kingdom of God.

NOTES

Chapter 1: The System of Civil Government

1. Romans 14:12, Matthew 16:27, Revelation 20:11–15 each emphasize God holding mankind individually responsible to Him.
2. *Strong's Exhaustive Concordance*, #3068.
3. For further reading on biblical justice, see the author's book *Oneness Embraced* (Moody, 2011).
4. To learn more about the kingdom agenda, see the author's volume *The Kingdom Agenda: What a Way to Live!* (Moody, 2006).

Chapter 2: The Sacred and the Secular

1. For further reading on God's kingdom, His values, and their application in society as outlined in Scripture, see the author's book *The Kingdom Agenda: What a Way to Live!* (Moody, 2006).

Chapter 3: Is God a Democrat or a Republican?

1. For further reading on the call to unity, see the author's work *Oneness Embraced: Through the Eyes of Tony Evans* (Moody, 2011).
2. While America was never formally established as a Christian nation—since neither God, the Bible, nor Jesus Christ are identified in the Constitution—the foundation on which the constitution was built included an acknowledgment of God's creative powers and rule through the Declaration of Independence. Likewise, America's culture was dominated by the influence of the Christian faith at that time.

THE URBAN ALTERNATIVE
The National Ministry of Dr. Tony Evans

Dr. Tony Evans and The Urban Alternative (TUA) equips, **empowers**, and **unites** Christians to **impact** *individuals, families, churches,* and *communities* for restoring hope and transforming lives.

We believe the core cause of the problems we face in our personal lives, homes, and societies is a spiritual one; therefore, the only way to address them is spiritually. We've tried a political, a social, an economic, and even a religious agenda. It's time for a Kingdom Agenda—God's visible and comprehensive rule over every area of life because when we function as we were designed, there is a divine power that changes everything. It renews and restores as the life of Christ is made manifest within our own. As we align ourselves under Him, there is an alignment that happens from deep within—where He brings about full restoration. It is an atmosphere that revives and makes whole.

As it impacts us, it impacts others, transforming every sphere of life in which we live. When each biblical sphere of life functions in accordance with God's Word, the outcomes are evangelism, discipleship, and community impact. As we learn how to govern ourselves under God, we then transform the institutions of family, church, and society from a biblically based kingdom perspective. Through Him, we are touching heaven and changing earth.

To achieve our goal we use a variety of strategies, methods, and resources for reaching and equipping as many people as possible.

BROADCAST MEDIA

Hundreds of thousands of individuals experience *The Alternative with Dr. Tony Evans* through the daily radio broadcast playing on more than **500 Radio Stations** and in more than **40 countries**. The broadcast can also be seen on several television networks, and is viewable online at TonyEvans.org.

LEADERSHIP TRAINING

Kingdom Agenda Pastors (KAP) provides a *viable network* for *like-minded pastors* who embrace the Kingdom Agenda philosophy. Pastors have the opportunity to go deeper with Dr. Tony Evans as they are given greater biblical knowledge, practical applications, and resources to impact individuals, families, churches, and communities. KAP welcomes *senior and associate pastors* of all churches.

The Kingdom Agenda Pastors Summit progressively develops church leaders to meet the demands of the 21st century while maintaining the Gospel message and the strategic position of the church. The Summit introduces *intensive seminars, workshops,* and *resources*— addressing issues affecting the community, family, leadership, organizational health, and more.

Pastors' Wives Ministry, founded by Dr. Lois Evans, provides *counsel, encouragement,* and *spiritual resources* for pastors' wives as they serve with their husbands in the ministry. A primary focus of the ministry is the KAP Summit that offers senior pastors' wives a safe place to *reflect, renew,* and *relax* along with training in personal development, spiritual growth, and care for their emotional and physical well-being.

COMMUNITY IMPACT

National Church Adopt-A-School Initiative (NCAASI) prepares churches across the country to impact communities by using *public schools as the primary vehicle for effecting positive social change* in urban youth and families. Leaders of churches, school districts, faith-based organizations, and other nonprofit organizations are equipped with the knowledge and tools to *forge partnerships* and build *strong social service delivery systems.* This training is based on the comprehensive church-based community impact strategy conducted by Oak Cliff Bible Fellowship. It addresses such areas as economic development, education, housing, health revitalization, family renewal, and racial reconciliation. We also assist churches in tailoring the model to meet the specific needs of their communities while simultaneously addressing the spiritual and moral frame of reference within the community.

Resource Development

We are fostering lifelong learning partnerships with the people we serve by providing a variety of published materials. We offer booklets, Bible studies, books, CDs, and DVDs to strengthen people in their walk with God and ministry to others.

For more information, a catalog of Dr. Tony Evans's ministry resources, and a complimentary copy of Dr. Evans's devotional newsletter, call (800) 800-3222 or write TUA at P.O. Box 4000, Dallas TX 75208, *or* log on to TonyEvans.org